DECORATED
gingerbread

DECORATED
gingerbread

annie rigg

photography by Tara Fisher

RYLAND
PETERS
& SMALL

LONDON NEW YORK

dedication

To Hattie & Albie and their fabulous dinosaur cookies!

Senior Designers Barbara Zuniga and Toni Kay
Senior Editor Céline Hughes
Production Toby Marshall
Art Director Leslie Harrington
Publishing Director Alison Starling

Prop Stylist Liz Belton
Indexer Sandra Shotter

Author's acknowledgements
Thank you to Tara for her utterly gorgeous pictures
and for allowing me to cover her kitchen with icing
sugar and food colouring. And to Alison Starling for
asking me to write my first book 3 years ago and for
never quite allowing me to put away the piping bags
and food colouring.

First published in 2011
by Ryland Peters & Small
20–21 Jockey's Fields
London WC1R 4BW
and
519 Broadway, 5th Floor
New York, NY 10012
www.rylandpeters.com

10 9 8 7 6 5 4 3 2 1

Text © Annie Rigg 2011
Design and photographs
© Ryland Peters & Small 2011

Printed in China

UK ISBN: 978-1-84975-145-2
US ISBN: 978-1-84975-189-6

A catalogue record for this book is available from the
British Library.

Library of Congress Cataloging-in-Publication Data

Rigg, Annie.
  Decorated gingerbread / Annie Rigg ; photography
by Tara Fisher.
       p. cm.
  Includes index.
  ISBN 978-1-84975-189-6
  1. Cake decorating. 2. Gingerbread. I. Title.
  TX771.2.R48 2011
  641.8'6539–dc23

                                   2011018398

Notes
• All spoon measurements are level unless otherwise
specified.
• Eggs used in the recipes in this book are large
unless otherwise specified.
• Ovens should be preheated to the specified
temperatures. All ovens work slightly differently. We
recommend using an oven thermometer and suggest
you consult the maker's handbook for any special
instructions, particularly if you are cooking in a fan-
assisted oven, as you will need to adjust temperatures
according to manufacturer's instructions.

contents

Here is a simple, spiced gingerbread dough suitable for all the decorated cookies in this book. The recipe makes approximately 12 medium-sized cookies depending on the cutters used. If you like, add 1 tablespoon finely chopped crystallized ginger or candied peel to the dough to make the gingerbread more sophisticated.

basic spiced gingerbread

2 tablespoons golden syrup

1 large egg yolk

200 g/1⅔ cups plain/all-purpose flour, plus extra for dusting

½ teaspoon baking powder

1½ teaspoons ground ginger

1 teaspoon ground cinnamon

¼ teaspoon freshly grated nutmeg

a pinch of salt

100 g/7 tablespoons unsalted butter, chilled and diced

75 g/⅓ cup light muscovado or light brown (soft) sugar

1. Beat together the golden syrup and egg yolk in a small bowl.

2. Sift the flour, baking powder, spices and salt into a food processor (or into a mixing bowl) and add the butter. Use the pulse button to process the mixture (or rub the butter into the flour mixture with your fingertips). When the mixture starts to look like sand and there are no lumps of butter, add the sugar and pulse (or mix with your fingers) again for 30 seconds to incorporate. With the motor running, add the egg-yolk mixture and pulse (or mix with a wooden spoon) until starting to clump together.

3. Tip the mixture out onto a very lightly floured surface and knead gently to bring together into a smooth ball. Flatten the dough into a disc, wrap in clingfilm/plastic wrap and refrigerate for 1–2 hours. Now go to Step 4 opposite.

This is a darker gingerbread dough with a hint of cocoa and a light smokiness from the treacle and dark brown sugar. The recipe will make approximately 12 cookies depending on the cutters used.

chocolate gingerbread

2 tablespoons golden syrup

2 tablespoons dark treacle/molasses

1 large egg yolk

200 g/1⅔ cups plain/all-purpose flour, plus extra for dusting

1 teaspoon baking powder

25 g/3 tablespoons cocoa powder

2 teaspoons ground ginger

½ teaspoon ground cinnamon

¼ teaspoon freshly grated nutmeg

a pinch of salt

75 g/5 tablespoons unsalted butter, chilled and diced

75 g/⅓ cup dark brown (soft) sugar

50 g/½ cup ground almonds

1. Beat together the golden syrup, treacle and egg yolk in a small bowl.

2. Sift the flour, baking powder, cocoa, spices and salt into a food processor (or into a mixing bowl) and add the butter. When the mixture starts to look like sand and there are no lumps of butter, add the sugar and almonds and pulse (or mix with your fingers) again for 30 seconds to incorporate. With the motor running, add the egg-yolk mixture and pulse (or mix with a wooden spoon) until starting to clump together.

3. Tip the mixture out onto a very lightly floured surface and knead gently to bring together into a smooth ball. Flatten the dough into a disc, wrap in clingfilm/plastic wrap and refrigerate for 1–2 hours.

4. Preheat the oven to 170˚C (325˚F) Gas 3.

5. Lightly dust a clean, dry surface with flour and roll the dough evenly to a thickness of 2–3 mm/⅛ inch. Use a cutter or template to stamp out as many cookies as possible from the dough, cutting each one as close as possible to the next one. Arrange the cookies on baking sheets lined with non-stick baking parchment.

6. Gather the dough scraps together, knead lightly, re-roll and stamp out more cookies until all the dough has been used up.

7. Bake the gingerbread in batches on the middle shelf of the preheated oven. Keep an eye on the cookies, as you want them to brown evenly. You may have to turn the baking sheets around if your oven is hotter on one side than the other.

8. Allow the cookies to cool completely on the baking sheets before icing. Store un-iced gingerbread cookies in an airtight container until needed.

royal icing

500 g/1 lb. royal icing sugar/mix

75–100 ml/⅓–½ cup cold water

OR

500 g/3⅓ cups icing/confectioners' sugar

2 large egg whites

Using royal icing sugar/mix

Tip the royal icing sugar/mix into a large mixing bowl and add the water gradually, mixing with a whisk or wooden spoon until the icing is smooth and thick enough that it will hold a ribbon trail when the spoon or whisk is lifted from the bowl. This will be the consistency that you need for piping outlines or details on the cookies. You may need to add slightly more or less water to achieve the right balance.

Using icing/confectioners' sugar

N.B. THIS METHOD USES RAW EGG

Follow the method above, but use the egg whites in place of the water.

Tinting icing

Divide the icing into separate bowls. I recommend using food colouring pastes for tinting royal icing. This is available in small pots and in a vast array of colours. A tiny amount of colouring goes a long way, so use it with caution. Using a cocktail stick/ toothpick, gradually add dots of colouring to the icing and mix well before adding more colour until you achieve the desired shade.

Preparing for piping

Fill the appropriate number of piping bags with enough icing to pipe any outlines or details – usually about 2 tablespoons. The remaining icing will be used for flooding the outlines and will need to be slightly runnier, so add a drop more water to make it more like the consistency of double/ heavy cream. Keep your icing covered when you're not using it to prevent it from drying out.

You will need piping bags to create the outlines and details on each cookie. I find that clear plastic disposable bags are the best thing for this purpose. They are readily available from good kitchenware shops, sugarcraft specialists and online suppliers and often come in packs of 24.

Flooding

Spoon the icing into the piping bag, squeeze the icing towards the tip and twist the top to prevent any icing leaking out. Using sharp scissors, snip a tiny point off the end of the bag. Carefully pipe a fine outline around the edge of each cookie in the shape that you require. Leave this to dry for at least 10 minutes before flooding the middle with the runnier icing. You can either do this with the piping bag again, or with a teaspoon or a tiny spatula. Make sure the icing evenly fills the outline.

Keep the filled icing bags wrapped in clingfilm/ plastic wrap when not in use so that the icing doesn't dry out.

Look for sets of teddy-bear cutters in assorted sizes so that you can make Papa, Mama and Baby bear cookies. I have made these brown teddy bears but you could turn them into polar bears if you prefer.

teddy bears

Basic Spiced Gingerbread (page 6)

plain/all-purpose flour, for rolling out

Royal Icing (page 9)

brown, black and pink food colouring pastes

teddy-bear cutters in 3 sizes

baking sheets, lined with non-stick baking parchment

disposable piping bags

makes 10-12

Prepare the Basic Spiced Gingerbread according to the recipe on page 6, stopping at the end of Step 3. Preheat the oven to 170°C (325°F) Gas 3.

Lightly dust a clean, dry surface with flour and roll the dough evenly to a thickness of 2–3 mm/⅛ inch. Use the cutters to stamp out as many cookies as possible from the dough, cutting each one as close as possible to the next one. Arrange the cookies on the prepared baking sheets. Gather the dough scraps together, knead lightly, re-roll and stamp out more cookies until all the dough has been used up. Bake the gingerbread in batches on the middle shelf of the preheated oven for 10–12 minutes or until firm and lightly browned at the edges. Allow the cookies to cool completely on the baking sheets before icing.

Prepare the Royal Icing according to the recipe on page 9. Put half the icing in one bowl, one quarter in a second bowl and the last quarter in a third bowl. Tint the largest bowl of icing light brown using the food colouring paste. Tint the second bowl black and the remaining bowl pink, cover and set aside.

Take 3 tablespoons of brown icing and add a little more colour to make it a deeper brown. Fill a

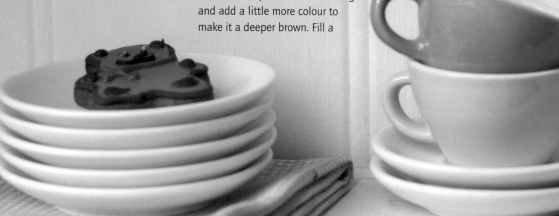

disposable piping bag with this darker colour and pipe outlines around the edge of each bear. (See page 9 for instructions on flooding.) Allow to dry for at least 10 minutes. Flood the insides of the outlines with paler brown icing. Allow to dry for 20 minutes. Pipe paws and ears onto each bear with the darker brown icing. Pipe the eyes, nose and mouth onto each bear using the black icing in another piping bag. Finish by putting the pink icing in another piping bag and piping a bow tie on each bear. Allow to dry completely before serving.

Basic Spiced Gingerbread (page 6)

plain/all-purpose flour, for rolling out

Royal Icing (page 9)

red, green, orange and black food colouring pastes

10–12 small red sugar-coated chocolate drops

edible sugar stars or mimosa balls

8–9-cm/3½-inch round cutter

baking sheets, lined with non-stick baking parchment

disposable piping bags

makes 10–12

These funny faces are made using a basic round cookie cutter and would be perfect for a children's birthday party.

kooky clowns

Prepare the Basic Spiced Gingerbread according to the recipe on page 6, stopping at the end of Step 3. Preheat the oven to 170°C (325°F) Gas 3.

Lightly dust a clean, dry surface with flour and roll the dough evenly to a thickness of 2–3 mm/⅛ inch. Use the cutters to stamp out as many cookies as possible from the dough, cutting each one as close as possible to the next one. Using a sharp knife, trim two thin slices off each gingerbread circle to make a triangular point – this will be the clown's hat. Arrange the cookies on the prepared baking sheets. Gather the dough scraps together, knead lightly, re-roll and stamp out more cookies until all the dough has been used up. Bake the gingerbread in batches on the middle shelf of the preheated oven for 10–12 minutes or until firm and lightly browned at the edges. Allow the cookies to cool completely on the baking sheets before icing.

Prepare the Royal Icing according to the recipe on page 9. Leave one third of the icing in the mixing bowl and divide the remaining icing between 3 small bowls. Using the food colouring pastes, tint one bowl of icing red, one green and one orange. Fill 4 disposable piping bags with 2 tablespoons of each icing. Start by piping the triangular outline of the clown's hat in either red or green. (See page 9 for instructions on flooding.) Pipe the outline for the hair in the orange icing, creating waves along the bottom. Using the white icing, pipe the outline for the face on the bottom half of the cookie. Tint 2 teaspoons of the white icing black. Allow the outlines to dry for at least 10 minutes. Flood the insides of the outlines with the corresponding icing. Allow to dry for 20 minutes.

Pipe patterns on the hats and curls in the hair. Adorn the hats with dots of icing and pop a star or mimosa ball at the top. Pipe a red smile and black crosses for eyes. Stick a red chocolate drop as a nose. Allow to dry completely before serving.

Dog-shaped cookie cutters are available in just about every shape and breed imaginable. I like the terrier-shaped cutters, as they seem more comical. Besides, my dog Mungo wouldn't approve of any other shape.

give a dog a bone

Prepare the Basic Spiced Gingerbread according to the recipe on page 6, stopping at the end of Step 3. Preheat the oven to 170°C (325°F) Gas 3.

Lightly dust a clean, dry surface with flour and roll the dough evenly to a thickness of 2–3 mm/⅛ inch. Use the cutters to stamp out as many cookies as possible from the dough, cutting each one as close as possible to the next one. Arrange the cookies on the prepared baking sheets. Gather the dough scraps together, knead lightly, re-roll and stamp out more cookies until all the dough has been used up. Bake the gingerbread in batches on the middle shelf of the preheated oven for 10–12 minutes or until firm and lightly browned at the edges. Allow the cookies to cool completely on the baking sheets before icing.

Prepare the Royal Icing according to the recipe on page 9. Leave one half of the icing in the mixing bowl and divide the remaining icing between 2 small bowls. Using the food colouring pastes, tint one bowl of icing brown and one black. Take out 1 tablespoon of icing from the white icing and tint this blue or red for the collars. Cover and set aside.

Fill a disposable piping bag with 2 tablespoons of the white icing. Pipe outlines around the edge of each bone and white-coloured dog. (See page 9 for instructions on flooding.) Fill 2 other piping bags with brown and black icings and pipe outlines for any brown- or black-coloured dogs. Allow to dry for at least 10 minutes, then flood the insides of the outlines with the corresponding icing. If your dogs have patches of colour, you need to do this before the icing sets. Add patches of brown and black to the white terriers. Allow to dry for 20 minutes.

Finally, pipe eyes and blue or red collars onto each dog. Decorate each collar with silver balls. Allow to dry completely before serving.

Basic Spiced Gingerbread (page 6)
plain/all-purpose flour, for rolling out
Royal Icing (page 9)
brown, black, blue/red food colouring
 pastes
edible silver balls

bone cutter and 2 or 3 assorted dog-shaped
 cutters
baking sheets, lined with non-stick baking
 parchment
disposable piping bags

makes 10–12

These pretty tags look gorgeous attached to gifts for a birthday. They also look special for a wedding as personalized place cards. You don't need special cookie cutters – just cut out a gift-tag template from card.

gift tags

Chocolate Gingerbread (page 7)
plain/all-purpose flour, for rolling out
Royal Icing (page 9)
pink and blue food colouring pastes

a piece of card to make a paper template
wooden skewer or cocktail stick/toothpick
disposable piping bags
short lengths of fine ribbon

makes 10–12

Prepare the Chocolate Gingerbread according to the recipe on page 7, stopping at the end of Step 3. Preheat the oven to 170°C (325°F) Gas 3.

Using the piece of card, cut out a gift-tag shaped template: cut out a rectangle roughly 12 x 7 cm/5 x 3 inches. Snip small triangles off the top 2 corners of the rectangle to make a tag shape. Lightly dust a clean, dry surface with flour and roll the dough evenly to a thickness of 2–3 mm/⅛ inch. Use the template to cut out as many cookies as possible from the dough, cutting each one as close as possible to the next one. Arrange the cookies on the prepared baking sheets. Gather the dough scraps together, knead lightly, re-roll and stamp out more cookies until all the dough has been used up. Using a wooden skewer or cocktail stick/toothpick, make a hole in the top of each tag so that you can thread a ribbon through it once it is iced. Bake the gingerbread in batches on the middle shelf of the preheated oven for 10–12 minutes or until firm and browned at the edges. You may need to reshape the hole for the ribbon using the skewer again. Allow the cookies to cool completely on the baking sheets before icing.

Prepare the Royal Icing according to the recipe on page 9. Leave 3 tablespoons of the icing in the mixing bowl and divide the remaining icing between 2 small bowls. Using the food colouring pastes, tint one bowl of icing pink and one blue. Fill one disposable piping bag with the white icing. Pipe outlines around the edge of each cookie. (See page 9 for instructions on flooding.) Allow to dry for at least 10 minutes. Flood the insides of the outlines with either pink or blue icing and allow to dry for 20 minutes. Tint the remaining pink and blue icings a slightly darker shade and spoon each into a new piping bag. Pipe decorative lines and dots around each gift tag. Finally, pipe the initial of each person into the middle of the tag and allow the icing to set completely before threading with fine ribbon and attaching to a parcel.

Purrrfect for Halloween or any other witchey-themed occasion. Look for different shapes of cat cutters and edible Halloween sprinkles in green, orange and black in cake-decorating stores or online suppliers.

witches' cats & hats

Prepare the Gingerbread according to the recipe on page 6–7, stopping at the end of Step 3. Preheat the oven to 170°C (325°F) Gas 3.

Lightly dust a clean, dry surface with flour and roll the dough evenly to a thickness of 2–3 mm/⅛ inch. Use the cutters to stamp out as many cookies as possible from the dough, cutting each one as close as possible to the next one. Arrange the cookies on the prepared baking sheets. Gather the dough scraps together, knead lightly, re-roll and stamp out more cookies until all the dough has been used up. Bake the gingerbread in batches on the middle shelf of the preheated oven for 10–12 minutes or until firm and browned at the edges. Allow the cookies to cool completely on the baking sheets before icing.

Prepare the Royal Icing according to the recipe on page 9. Leave 2 teaspoons of the icing in the mixing bowl, cover and set aside. Put 3–4 tablespoons in a small bowl and tint this green using the food colouring paste. Cover and set aside. Tint the remaining icing black.

Fill a disposable piping bag with the black icing and pipe a fine line around the edge of each cookie. (See page 9 for instructions on flooding.) Allow to dry for at least 10 minutes.

Flood the insides of the outlines with black icing. Tip the orange and black sprinkles into a saucer and dip the bottom edge of each hat in the sprinkles. Allow to dry for 20 minutes.

Fill another piping bag with the reserved green icing and pipe a green band around each hat and a collar on each cat. Carefully sprinkle orange and green sanding sugar on the hat bands. Give each cat a set of white eyes and dot with a little black icing. Allow to dry completely before serving.

Basic Spiced or Chocolate Gingerbread (page 6–7)

plain/all-purpose flour, for rolling out

Royal Icing (page 9)

green and black food colouring pastes

orange and black sprinkles

orange and green sanding sugar

cat and witches'-hat cutters

baking sheets, lined with non-stick baking parchment

disposable piping bags

makes 10–12

These wide-eyed creatures require no fancy cookie cutters – just plain round cutters in assorted sizes. I have made these into brown owls but there's no reason why they couldn't be tawny or even snowy owls.

a parliament of owls

Basic Spiced Gingerbread (page 6)
plain/all-purpose flour, for rolling out
Royal Icing (page 9)
brown, black and yellow food colouring pastes

assorted round cutters between 6 cm/ 2½ inches and 8 cm/7¼ inches
baking sheets, lined with non-stick baking parchment
disposable piping bags

makes 10–12

Prepare the Basic Spiced Gingerbread according to the recipe on page 6, stopping at the end of Step 3. Preheat the oven to 170°C (325°F) Gas 3.

Lightly dust a clean, dry surface with flour and roll the dough evenly to a thickness of 2–3 mm/⅛ inch. Use the cutters to stamp out as many cookies as possible from the dough, cutting each one as close as possible to the next one. Arrange the cookies on the prepared baking sheets. Gather the dough scraps together, knead lightly, re-roll and stamp out more cookies until all the dough has been used up. Bake the gingerbread in batches on the middle shelf of the preheated oven for 10–12 minutes or until firm and lightly browned at the edges. Allow the cookies to cool completely on the baking sheets before icing.

Prepare the Royal Icing according to the recipe on page 9. Leave 3 tablespoons of the icing in the mixing bowl, cover and set aside. Put 2 tablespoons in a small bowl and tint this yellow using the food colouring paste. Tint another 2 tablespoons black. Cover and set aside. Tint the remaining icing brown.

Fill a disposable piping bag with 3 tablespoons of the brown icing and pipe the outline of an owl on each cookie. (See page 9 for instructions on flooding.) Allow to dry for at least 10 minutes.

Flood the insides of the outlines with brown icing. Allow to dry for 20 minutes.

Colour the remaining brown icing a deeper shade of brown, spoon into a piping bag and pipe fine feathers in swirly rows over the owls' bodies. Fill another piping bag with the reserved black icing and pipe 2 circles for the eyes. Allow to set, then flood with white icing. Using the tip of a knife, make a triangular beak and feet with the reserved yellow icing. Complete the eyes with black dots. Allow to dry completely before serving perched on tree branches.

Basic Spiced or Chocolate Gingerbread (page 6–7)

plain/all-purpose flour, for rolling out

Royal Icing (page 9)

black, red, blue and green food colouring pastes

assorted car cutters

baking sheets, lined with non-stick baking parchment

disposable piping bags

makes 10–12

If, like me, you know little boys (and men) that are car crazy, these are sure to please. Cookie cutters in the shapes of cars are now available in all shapes and sizes, from Ferraris to Beetles.

racing cars

Prepare the Gingerbread according to the recipe on page 6–7, stopping at the end of Step 3. Preheat the oven to 170°C (325°F) Gas 3.

Lightly dust a clean, dry surface with flour and roll the dough evenly to a thickness of 2–3 mm/⅛ inch. Use the cutters to stamp out as many cookies as possible from the dough, cutting each one as close as possible to the next one. Arrange the cookies on the prepared baking sheets. Gather the dough scraps together, knead lightly, re-roll and stamp out more cookies until all the dough has been used up. Bake the gingerbread in batches on the middle shelf of the preheated oven for 10–12 minutes or until firm and browned at the edges. Allow the cookies to cool completely on the baking sheets before icing.

Prepare the Royal Icing according to the recipe on page 9. Leave 2 teaspoons of the icing in the mixing bowl, cover and set aside. Put 4 tablespoons in a small bowl and tint black using the food colouring paste. Divide the remaining icing between 3 bowls and tint one bowl red, one blue and one green. Spoon 2 tablespoons of each into a disposable piping bag and pipe outlines around each cookie, leaving space for the wheels. (See page 9 for instructions on flooding.) Fill another piping bag with the black icing and pipe outlines for the wheels. Allow to dry for at least 10 minutes.

Flood the insides of the car and wheel outlines with the corresponding icing. Allow to dry for 20 minutes.

Pipe fine lines for the doors onto each car and number each car in a contrasting colour. Pipe hubcaps, headlights, door handles and any other details with the reserved white icing. Allow to dry completely before serving.

Every flock should have just one black sheep amongst all the snowy white lambs. Make a batch of these adorable chocolate gingerbread cookies for Easter instead of buying in some chocolate eggs.

flock of fluffy sheep

Prepare the Chocolate Gingerbread according to the recipe on page 7, stopping at the end of Step 3. Preheat the oven to 170˚C (325˚F) Gas 3.

Lightly dust a clean, dry surface with flour and roll the dough evenly to a thickness of 2-3 mm/⅛ inch. Use the cutters to stamp out as many cookies as possible from the dough, cutting each one as close as possible to the next one. Arrange the cookies on the prepared baking sheets. Gather the dough scraps together, knead lightly, re-roll and stamp out more cookies until all the dough has been used up. Bake the gingerbread in batches on the middle shelf of the preheated oven for 10–12 minutes or until firm and browned at the edges. Allow the cookies to cool completely on the baking sheets before icing.

Prepare the Royal Icing according to the recipe on page 9. Take out 1 tablespoon and tint pink using the food colouring paste. Cover and set aside. Take another 2 tablespoons of the icing and tint black for the one black sheep of the flock. Cover and set aside. Put the remaining, white icing in one of the disposable piping bags and pipe outlines around the edges of all but one of the sheep. (See page 9 for instructions on flooding.) Allow to dry for at least 10 minutes.

Flood the insides of the outlines with white icing. Allow to dry for 20 minutes.

Use the black icing to make legs, eyes and a nose on each sheep. Thicken the remaining white icing slightly by beating it vigorously for a minute or by adding more icing/confectioners' sugar. Pipe woolly squiggles over the body of the sheep and, using the tip of a knife or a teaspoon, give each sheep pink ears.

Make the black sheep using the method above and allow to dry completely before serving.

Chocolate Gingerbread (page 7)
plain/all-purpose flour, for rolling out
Royal Icing (page 9)
pink and black food colouring pastes

sheep cutters
baking sheets, lined with non-stick baking parchment
disposable piping bags

makes 10–12

Use an extra-large gingerbread-man cutter for these scoundrels and simply shape one of the legs into a peg leg with a sharp knife. If you were feeling adventurous, you could make a pirate ship cake for this rabble of pirates to sail the high seas in.

long john silver

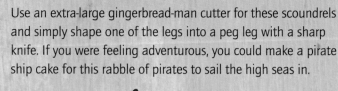

Prepare the Basic Spiced Gingerbread according to the recipe on page 6, stopping at the end of Step 3. Preheat the oven to 170˚C (325˚F) Gas 3.

Lightly dust a clean, dry surface with flour and roll the dough evenly to a thickness of 2–3 mm/ ⅛ inch. Use the cutters to stamp out as many cookies as possible from the dough, cutting each one as close as possible to the next one. Arrange the cookies on the prepared baking sheets. Gather the dough scraps together, knead lightly, re-roll and stamp out more cookies until all the dough has been used up. Using a small, sharp knife cut one of the legs on each man into a stump shape. Bake the gingerbread in batches on the middle shelf of the preheated oven for 10–12 minutes or until firm and lightly browned at the edges. Allow the cookies to cool completely on the baking sheets before icing.

Prepare the Royal Icing according to the recipe on page 9. Leave 1 teaspoon of the icing in the mixing bowl, cover and set aside. Spoon one quarter of the remaining icing into a small bowl and tint it black using food colouring paste. Divide the remaining icing between 3 bowls and tint one bowl red, one yellow and one blue.

Spoon 2 tablespoons of the blue icing into a disposable piping bag and pipe an outline for the pirates' trousers and his headscarf. Use the yellow icing to draw an outline for his T-shirt. Use the black icing to draw outlines for the boots and the peg leg. (See page 9 for instructions on flooding.) Allow to dry for at least 10 minutes.

Flood the insides of the outlines for the trousers and headscarf sections with the blue icing. Pipe red and yellow stripes across the T-shirt. Flood the boots and peg leg with black icing. Allow to dry for 20 minutes.

Pipe black icing across the pirate's waist to make a belt and position a yellow chocolate drop in the middle as a buckle. Give each pirate a black eye patch and pipe yellow polka dots onto the headscarf, plus a yellow button on the boot. Pipe a dot of white and black icing for the remaining eyes and give each pirate a red dastardly grin. Allow to dry completely before serving. Crocodile optional.

Basic Spiced Gingerbread (page 6)

plain/all-purpose flour, for rolling out

Royal Icing (page 9)

black, red, yellow and blue food colouring pastes

6 small yellow sugar-coated chocolate drops

20-cm/8-inch-tall gingerbread-man cutter

baking sheets, lined with non-stick baking parchment

disposable piping bags

makes about 6

Basic Spiced Gingerbread (page 6)
plain/all-purpose flour, for rolling out
½ quantity Royal Icing (page 9)
assorted sugar-coated chocolate drops

gingerbread-people cutters in assorted sizes
baking sheets, lined with non-stick baking
     parchment
a disposable piping bag

makes 10–12

As a child I loved gingerbread men – making them and eating them.
These simple shapes are great fun for children to decorate and the
classic cutters are widely available in all shapes and sizes. I have iced
them very simply on this occasion, but feel free to give this family
whatever clothes you like! I have used sugar-coated chocolate drops
for buttons but the more traditional decoration would be raisins.

gingerbread family

Prepare the Basic Spiced Gingerbread according to the recipe on page 6, stopping at the end of Step 3. Preheat the oven to 170°C (325°F) Gas 3.

Lightly dust a clean, dry surface with flour and roll the dough evenly to a thickness of 2–3 mm/⅛ inch. Use the cutters to stamp out as many cookies as possible from the dough, cutting each one as close as possible to the next one. Arrange the cookies on the prepared baking sheets. Gather the dough scraps together, knead lightly, re-roll and stamp out more cookies until all the dough has been used

up. Bake the gingerbread in batches on the middle shelf of the preheated oven for 10–12 minutes or until firm and lightly browned at the edges. Allow the cookies to cool completely on the baking sheets before icing.

Prepare the Royal Icing according to the recipe on page 9. Spoon the icing into a disposable piping bag. Pipe simple clothes and faces onto each cookie and decorate each person with colourful sugar-coated chocolate drops, stuck on with a small blob of icing. Allow to dry completely before serving.

The perfect cookie for a baking queen! Cookies and cupcakes all rolled into one and decorated with a generous swirl of 'frosting' and a scattering of sprinkles.

cupcake cookies

Prepare the Chocolate Gingerbread according to the recipe on page 7, stopping at the end of Step 3. Preheat the oven to 170°C (325°F) Gas 3.

Lightly dust a clean, dry surface with flour and roll the dough evenly to a thickness of 2–3 mm/⅛ inch. Use the cutters to stamp out as many cookies as possible from the dough, cutting each one as close as possible to the next one. Arrange the cookies on the prepared baking sheets. Gather the dough scraps together, knead lightly, re-roll and stamp out more cookies until all the dough has been used up. Bake the gingerbread in batches on the middle shelf of the preheated oven for 10–12 minutes or until firm and browned at the edges. Allow the cookies to cool completely on the baking sheets before icing.

Prepare the Royal Icing according to the recipe on page 9. Leave one quarter of the icing in the mixing bowl and divide the remaining icing between 3 bowls. Using the food colouring pastes, tint one bowl of icing yellow, one brown and one pink. Spoon 3 tablespoons of the yellow icing into a disposable piping bag. Take half the cookies and pipe outlines around the bottom half of each one in the shape of a cupcake case. (See page 9 for instructions on flooding.) Repeat this with the pink icing and the remaining cookies. Spoon 2 tablespoons of the brown icing into another piping bag and pipe outlines around the top of half the cookies to resemble cupcake frosting. Repeat with the white icing and remaining cookies. Allow to dry for 10 minutes. Flood the insides of the pink cupcake cases with yellow icing and the yellow cases with pink icing. Allow to dry for 20 minutes, then pipe vertical lines in contrasting colours. Thicken the remaining brown and white icings slightly by beating it vigorously for a minute or by adding icing/confectioners' sugar. Pipe squiggles and swirls on the top half of each cookie. Decorate with sprinkles and chocolate drops. Allow to dry completely before serving.

Chocolate Gingerbread (page 7)
plain/all-purpose flour, for rolling out
Royal Icing (page 9)
yellow, brown and pink food colouring pastes
chocolate sprinkles
hundreds and thousands/jimmies
assorted candy-coated chocolate drops

assorted cupcake cutters
baking sheets, lined with non-stick baking parchment
disposable piping bags

makes 10–12

Cookie cutters are available in a variety of nautical shapes. Take your pick! Serve these cookies on a beach of edible sand (finely crushed plain cookies), fill a small bucket and have the cookies tumbling out.

she sells seashells

Basic Spiced Gingerbread (page 6)
plain/all-purpose flour, for rolling out
Royal Icing (page 9)
red, brown and blue food colouring pastes
edible sugar pearls

seashell, starfish and anchor cutters
baking sheets, lined with non-stick baking parchment
disposable piping bags

makes 10–12

Prepare the Basic Spiced Gingerbread according to the recipe on page 6, stopping at the end of Step 3. Preheat the oven to 170°C (325°F) Gas 3.

Lightly dust a clean, dry surface with flour and roll the dough evenly to a thickness of 2–3 mm/⅛ inch. Use the cutters to stamp out as many cookies as possible from the dough, cutting each one as close as possible to the next one. Arrange the cookies on the prepared baking sheets. Gather the dough scraps together, knead lightly, re-roll and stamp out more cookies until all the dough has been used up. Bake the gingerbread in batches on the middle shelf of the preheated oven for 10–12 minutes or until firm and lightly browned at the edges. Allow the cookies to cool completely on the baking sheets before icing.

Prepare the Royal Icing according to the recipe on page 9. Put 2 tablespoons of the icing into a small bowl and tint red using the food colouring paste. Spoon it into a disposable piping bag and pipe outlines around the edges of the starfish shapes. (See page 9 for instructions on flooding.) Transfer another 2 tablespoons of the icing into a small bowl and tint a very pale brown. Pipe a fine outline around the shell shapes. Reserve the remaining red and brown icings for later. Transfer another 2 tablespoons of the icing into a bowl and tint blue. Cover and set aside. Put the remaining icing into another piping bag and pipe outlines around the anchor shapes. Allow to dry for at least 10 minutes. Tint one third of the remaining icing pale pink using a tiny dot of the red paste, colour another third of the icing pale ivory using the brown paste and leave the remaining third white. Flood the starfish cookies with the pink icing, the shells with the ivory and the anchors with the white. Allow to dry for 20 minutes.

Tint the remaining white icing blue and use this and the reserved red icing to pipe details on the anchors. Use the reserved brown icing to pipe ridges on each shell and decorate with a sugar pearl. Allow to dry completely before serving.

Why not give a box of these fantastically girly cookies to your mum on Mother's Day to let her know just how much she means to you? They'd also be perfect to serve at a very pink-themed engagement party!

love hearts

Prepare the Gingerbread according to the recipe on page 6–7, stopping at the end of Step 3. Preheat the oven to 170°C (325°F) Gas 3.

Lightly dust a clean, dry surface with flour and roll the dough evenly to a thickness of 2–3 mm/⅛ inch. Use the cutters to stamp out as many cookies as possible from the dough, cutting each one as close as possible to the next one. Arrange the cookies on the prepared baking sheets. Gather the dough scraps together, knead lightly, re-roll and stamp out more cookies until all the dough has been used up. Bake the gingerbread in batches on the middle shelf of the preheated oven for 10–12 minutes or until firm and browned at the edges. Allow the cookies to cool completely on the baking sheets before icing.

Prepare the Royal Icing according to the recipe on page 9. Leave one third of the icing in the mixing bowl and transfer the rest to another bowl. Tint pale pink using the food colouring paste. Fill a disposable piping bag with 2 tablespoons of the pink icing. Take some of the cookies and pipe pink outlines around each one. (See page 9 for instructions on flooding.) Take another piping bag and fill with the white icing. Use to pipe outlines around the remaining cookies. Allow the icing to set for 10 minutes. Flood the insides of the outlines with the corresponding colour. Allow to dry for 20 minutes. Add food colouring to the pink icing and use this or the remaining white icing to pipe delicate lines, dots and rosettes (using the star-shaped nozzle/tip) around the edges and in the middle of each cookie. Now add more colouring to make a deeper pink and pipe more details on the cookies. Allow to dry completely before serving.

Basic Spiced or Chocolate Gingerbread
   (page 6–7)
plain/all-purpose flour, for rolling out
Royal Icing (page 9)
pink food colouring paste

heart cutters in assorted sizes
baking sheets, lined with non-stick baking
   parchment
disposable piping bags
small star-shaped piping nozzle/tip

makes 10–12

If you can find leaf cutters, great, but if not, it's very simple to make your own leaf shapes. I make a template for the more intricate leaves and cut the simpler leaves free-form using a small, sharp knife.

autumn leaves

Prepare the Gingerbread according to the recipe on page 6-7, stopping at the end of Step 3. Preheat the oven to 170°C (325°F) Gas 3.

If you are making a template, draw a 10–12-cm/4–5-inch maple leaf shape onto a piece of card and cut it out.

Lightly dust a clean, dry surface with flour and roll the dough evenly to a thickness of 2–3 mm/⅛ inch. Use the leaf cutters or the template to cut out 4 maple leaves, cutting each one as close as possible to the next one. Cut the simpler leaf shapes free-form using a small, sharp knife. Arrange the cookies on the prepared baking sheets. Gather the dough scraps together, knead lightly, re-roll and stamp out more cookies until all the dough has been used up. Bake the gingerbread in batches on the middle shelf of the preheated oven for 10–12 minutes or until firm and browned at the edges. Allow the cookies to cool completely on the baking sheets before icing.

Prepare the Royal Icing according to the recipe on page 9. Divide the icing between 3 or 4 bowls and tint each bowl a different shade of brown or copper using the food colouring pastes. Spoon 2–3 tablespoons of each colour into separate disposable piping bags. Pipe outlines around the edge of each cookie, making sure that you have a good assortment of colours. (See page 9 for instructions on flooding.) Allow the icing to set for 10 minutes.

Flood the insides of the outlines with a contrasting colour. Allow to dry for 20 minutes.

Pipe fine veining over the leaves in the same colour that you used for the outline. Allow to dry completely before serving.

Basic Spiced or Chocolate Gingerbread
(page 6-7)
plain/all-purpose flour, for rolling out
Royal Icing (page 9)
brown and copper food colouring pastes

assorted leaf cutters or a piece of card to
    make a paper template
baking sheets, lined with non-stick baking
    parchment
disposable piping bags

makes 10-12

This little princess is dressed in a confection of pink frills and her coronet is complete with sparkling jewels. Use a regular gingerbread-lady cutter and let your imagination go wild with her luxurious regal finery.

pink princess

Prepare the Basic Spiced Gingerbread according to the recipe on page 6, stopping at the end of Step 3. Preheat the oven to 170°C (325°F) Gas 3.

Lightly dust a clean, dry surface with flour and roll the dough evenly to a thickness of 2–3 mm/⅛ inch. Use the cutters to stamp out as many cookies as possible from the dough, cutting each one as close as possible to the next one. Arrange the cookies on the prepared baking sheets. Gather the dough scraps together, knead lightly, re-roll and stamp out more cookies until all the dough has been used up. Bake the gingerbread in batches on the middle shelf of the preheated oven for 10–12 minutes or until firm and lightly browned at the edges. Allow the cookies to cool completely on the baking sheets before icing.

Prepare the Royal Icing according to the recipe on page 9. Spoon 2 tablespoons of the icing into a small bowl and tint yellow using the food colouring paste. Cover and set aside. Tint another 2 tablespoons of the icing red, cover and set aside. Spoon 2 teaspoons of the white icing into a small bowl, cover and set aside. Tint the remaining icing into 2 different shades of pink. Fill a disposable piping bag with 2 tablespoons of the paler pink icing and pipe outlines in the shape of a dress around each cookie. (See page 9 for instructions on floodling.) Allow to dry for 10 minutes. Flood the insides of the dresses with the darker shade of pink. Allow to dry for 20 minutes.

Pipe decorative patterns and a sash over the dress using the reserved white and remaining pink icings. Finish the sash with a buckle made from a pink chocolate drop. Use the reserved red icing to give each princess a pair of dancing shoes and a big smile. Use the yellow icing to pipe a coronet and jewellery onto the cookies. Adorn the jewellery with edible gold balls. Pipe little eyes using white and black icing. Allow to dry completely before serving.

Basic Spiced Gingerbread (page 6)

plain/all-purpose flour, for rolling out

Royal Icing (page 9)

pink, red, yellow and black food colouring pastes

10–12 small pink candy-coated chocolate drops

small edible gold balls

gingerbread-lady cutter

baking sheets, lined with non-stick baking parchment

disposable piping bags

makes 10–12

For this school-themed recipe I used large, numbered cookies but you could just as easily use large letter shapes or even a mixture of both.

spotty numbers

Prepare the Basic Spiced Gingerbread according to the recipe on page 6, stopping at the end of Step 3. Preheat the oven to 170°C (325°F) Gas 3.

Lightly dust a clean, dry surface with flour and roll the dough evenly to a thickness of 2–3 mm/⅛ inch. Use the cutters to stamp out as many cookies as possible from the dough, cutting each one as close as possible to the next one. Arrange the cookies on the prepared baking sheets. Gather the dough scraps together, knead lightly, re-roll and stamp out more cookies until all the dough has been used up. Bake the gingerbread in batches on the middle shelf of the preheated oven for 10–12 minutes or until firm and lightly browned at the edges. Allow the cookies to cool completely on the baking sheets before icing.

Prepare the Royal Icing according to the recipe on page 9. Divide the icing between 4 bowls. Using the food colouring pastes tint one bowl of icing yellow, one baby-blue and one baby-pink. Cover each bowl and set aside. Leave the remaining bowl of icing white. Spoon the white icing into a disposable piping bag and pipe outlines around each cookie. (See page 9 for instructions on flooding.) Allow to dry for 10 minutes.

Flood the insides of the outlines with either the yellow, blue or pink icing and allow to dry for no more than 5 minutes. Pipe small dots of white icing onto each cookie. Allow to dry completely before serving.

Basic Spiced Gingerbread (page 6)
plain/all-purpose flour, for rolling out
Royal Icing (page 9)
yellow, blue and pink food colouring pastes

10-cm/4-inch numbered cutters
baking sheets, lined with non-stick baking parchment
disposable piping bags

makes 10–12

My grandparents used to have a tea service in a very similar blue and white pattern as these cookies. Why not take inspiration from your china and decorate your cookies to match?

time for tea

Prepare the Basic Spiced Gingerbread according to the recipe on page 6, stopping at the end of Step 3. Preheat the oven to 170˚C (325˚F) Gas 3.

Lightly dust a clean, dry surface with flour and roll the dough evenly to a thickness of 2–3 mm/⅛ inch. Use the cutters to stamp out as many cookies as possible from the dough, cutting each one as close as possible to the next one. Arrange the cookies on the prepared baking sheets. Gather the dough scraps together, knead lightly, re-roll and stamp out more cookies until all the dough has been used up. Bake the gingerbread in batches on the middle shelf of the preheated oven for 10–12 minutes or until firm and lightly browned at the edges. Allow the cookies to cool completely on the baking sheets before icing.

Prepare the Royal Icing according to the recipe on page 9. Leave two thirds of the icing in the mixing bowl and transfer the rest to another bowl. Tint this pale blue using the food colouring paste. Fill a disposable piping bag with the blue icing and pipe outlines around the edge of each cookie. (See page 9 for instructions on flooding.) Allow to dry for 10 minutes.

Flood the insides of the outlines with white icing. Allow to dry for 20 minutes, then pipe delicate patterns over the teacups and teapots. Allow to dry completely before serving.

Basic Spiced Gingerbread (page 6)
plain/all-purpose flour, for rolling out
Royal Icing (page 9)
blue food colouring paste

teapot and teacup cutters
baking sheets, lined with non-stick baking parchment
disposable piping bags

makes 10–12

Basic Spiced Gingerbread (page 6)
plain/all-purpose flour, for rolling out
Royal Icing (page 9)
green, red, yellow and purple food
    colouring pastes

10-cm/4-inch tulip cutters
baking sheets, lined with non-stick baking
    parchment
disposable piping bags
wooden skewer or cocktail stick/toothpick

makes 16–20

I have used a tulip cutter for these floral delights but if you can't get one, use whichever flower shapes you can find. Wrap the finished cookies in cellophane and tie with ribbons to make a cookie bouquet.

tulip garden

Prepare the Basic Spiced Gingerbread according to the recipe on page 6, stopping at the end of Step 3. Preheat the oven to 170°C (325°F) Gas 3.

Lightly dust a clean, dry surface with flour and roll the dough evenly to a thickness of 2–3 mm/⅛ inch. Use the cutters to stamp out as many cookies as possible from the dough, cutting each one as close as possible to the next one. Arrange the cookies on the prepared baking sheets. Gather the dough scraps together, knead lightly, re-roll and stamp out more cookies until all the dough has been used up. Bake the gingerbread in batches on the middle shelf of the preheated oven for 10–12 minutes or until firm and lightly browned at the edges. Allow the cookies to cool completely on the baking sheets before icing.

Prepare the Royal Icing according to the recipe on page 9. Take out 2 teaspoons of the icing, cover and set aside. Spoon half the remaining icing into another bowl and tint green using the food colouring paste. Divide the remaining icing between 3 bowls and tint one bowl red, one yellow and one purple. Fill a disposable piping bag with 3 tablespoons of the green icing and pipe outlines around the stalk and leaves of each cookie. Repeat this technique with a further 3 piping bags filled with the red, yellow and purple icing to make the petal part of the tulips. (See page 9 for instructions on flooding.) Allow the icing to set for 10 minutes.

Flood the insides of the outlines with the corresponding colour. To make a feather effect on the petals, pipe dots of contrasting icing (including the reserved white) along the bottom edge of each flower head and, using a wooden skewer or cocktail stick/toothpick, drag the dots of icing upward to gently mix the colours. Allow to dry for 20 minutes. Using the green icing, pipe fine veining over the leaves. Allow to dry completely before serving.

I was shown some rather splendid flamenco shoes when I asked two little girls how I should decorate these cookies. So here they are – edible dancing shoes as worn (and eaten) by Liliana and Saskia. Shoe cutters come in all shapes, sizes and styles, so go for your favourites.

dancing shoes

Prepare the Basic Spiced Gingerbread according to the recipe on page 6, stopping at the end of Step 3. Preheat the oven to 170°C (325°F) Gas 3.

Lightly dust a clean, dry surface with flour and roll the dough evenly to a thickness of 2–3 mm/⅛ inch. Use the cutters to stamp out as many cookies as possible from the dough, cutting each one as close as possible to the next one. Arrange the cookies on the prepared baking sheets. Gather the dough scraps together, knead lightly, re-roll and stamp out more cookies until all the dough has been used up. Bake the gingerbread in batches on the middle shelf of the preheated oven for 10–12 minutes or until firm and lightly browned at the edges. Allow the cookies to cool completely on the baking sheets before icing.

Prepare the Royal Icing according to the recipe on page 9. Leave one quarter of the icing in the mixing bowl and divide the remaining icing between 2 bowls. Using the food colouring pastes, tint one bowl of icing blue and one red. Cover the bowls and set aside.

Fill a disposable piping bag with the white icing and pipe outlines around the edge of each cookie. (See page 9 for instructions on flooding.) Allow to dry for 10 minutes.

Flood the insides of half the cookies with the reserved red icing and the other half with the blue icing and allow to dry for no more than 5 minutes. Pipe white dots onto each cookie. Embellish the shoes with sugar-coated chocolate drops. Allow to dry completely before serving.

Basic Spiced Gingerbread (page 6)
plain/all-purpose flour, for rolling out
Royal Icing (page 9)
blue and red food colouring pastes
small blue and red sugar-coated chocolate drops

high-heeled dancing-shoe cutter (about 10–12 cm/4–5 inches)
baking sheets, lined with non-stick baking parchment
disposable piping bags

makes 10–12

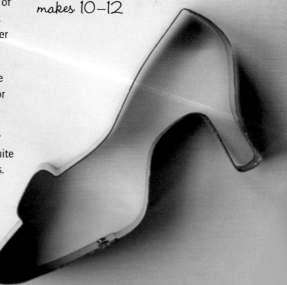

2 x Basic Spiced Gingerbread (page 6)
250 g/9 oz. clear, hard, fruit candies
plain/all-purpose flour, for rolling out
Royal Icing (page 9)

pieces of card to make paper templates
3 baking sheets, lined with non-stick baking
    parchment
disposable piping bag

makes a small village

This is a far simpler way of making a traditional gingerbread house.
Don't forget to make a sugar-paste snowman to finish the scene!

snowy village

Prepare the Basic Spiced Gingerbread according to the recipe on page 6,
stopping at the end of Step 3. Preheat the oven to 170°C (325°F) Gas 3.

Draw about 5 houses of your chosen shape and size onto pieces of card and cut
them out. The largest should be no bigger than about 20–30 cm/8–12 inches.

Divide the fruit candies into separate colours and place each colour in its own freezer bag. Using a rolling pin, crush the candies into small pieces.

Lightly dust a clean, dry surface with flour. Divide the dough into 5 pieces in sizes to correspond to the house sizes you have chosen. Roll the dough out into neat rectangles and use the templates to cut out the house shapes. Carefully slide the shapes onto the prepared baking sheets. Using a small, sharp knife or cutters, cut out windows from each house. Bake the houses in batches on the middle shelf of the preheated oven for about 5 minutes until the gingerbread is just starting to colour at the edges.

Remove the baking sheets from the oven. Carefully and neatly fill the windows with the crushed fruit candies using a dry pastry brush to brush away any stray candy pieces. Return the baking sheets to the oven and bake for a further 5 minutes until the gingerbread is golden brown and firm

festive

and the candies have melted to fill the window shapes. Allow the houses to cool completely on the baking sheets before icing.

Prepare the Royal Icing according to the recipe on page 9. Fill a disposable piping bag with the icing and pipe lines and dots around the windows and walls of each house. Pipe tiles onto the roofs. Allow to dry completely before serving. The houses look best displayed against a window so that the light shines through the 'stained-glass' windows.

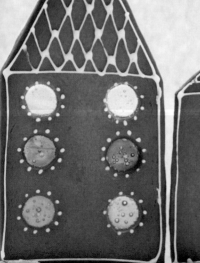

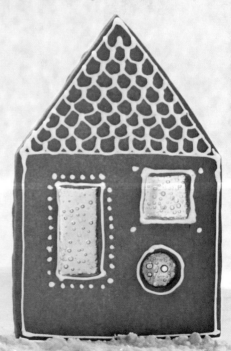

I have kept the decoration to a minimum on these stars, but add as much sparkle as you like. Once the icing has dried completely, you could serve the cookies in a towering stack as a table centrepiece.

christmas stars

Basic Spiced or Chocolate Gingerbread (page 6–7)

plain/all-purpose flour, for rolling out

Royal Icing (page 9)

yellow food colouring paste

edible gold glitter

silver sugar stars

edible silver balls

assorted star cutters

baking sheets, lined with non-stick baking parchment

disposable piping bags

makes 10–12

Prepare the Gingerbread according to the recipe on page 6–7, stopping at the end of Step 3. Preheat the oven to 170°C (325°F) Gas 3.

Lightly dust a clean, dry surface with flour and roll the dough evenly to a thickness of 2–3 mm/⅛ inch. Use the cutters to stamp out as many cookies as possible from the dough, cutting each one as close as possible to the next one. Arrange the cookies on the prepared baking sheets. Gather the dough scraps together, knead lightly, re-roll and stamp out more cookies until all the dough has been used up. Bake the gingerbread in batches on the middle shelf of the preheated oven for 10–12 minutes or until firm and browned at the edges. Allow the cookies to cool completely on the baking sheets before icing.

Prepare the Royal Icing according to the recipe on page 9. Transfer about 3 tablespoons to a small bowl and tint yellow using the food colouring paste. Spoon the yellow icing into a disposable piping bag and pipe outlines around each cookie. (See page 9 for instructions on flooding.) Allow the icing to set for 10 minutes.

Flood the insides of the outlines with the white icing. Allow to dry for 5 minutes before scattering edible glitter and sugar stars over the cookies. Pipe small dots of icing onto the point of each star and top with edible silver balls. Allow to dry completely before serving.

Festive ornament cutters are often sold in packs of 4–5 assorted shapes, ranging from the very simple to the more ornate. If you want to hang them from the Christmas tree, make a hole in the top before baking.

christmas ornaments

Prepare the Basic Spiced Gingerbread according to the recipe on page 6, stopping at the end of Step 3. Preheat the oven to 170°C (325°F) Gas 3.

Lightly dust a clean, dry surface with flour and roll the dough evenly to a thickness of 2–3 mm/⅛ inch. Use the cutters to stamp out as many cookies as possible from the dough, cutting each one as close as possible to the next one. Arrange the cookies on the prepared baking sheets. Gather the dough scraps together, knead lightly, re-roll and stamp out more cookies until all the dough has been used up. If you want to hang the ornaments on the Christmas tree later, use a wooden skewer or cocktail stick/toothpick to make a hole in the top of each cookie. Bake the gingerbread in batches on the middle shelf of the preheated oven for 10–12 minutes or until firm and lightly browned at the edges. You may need to reshape the hole for the ribbon using the skewer again. Allow the cookies to cool completely on the baking sheets before icing.

Prepare the Royal Icing according to the recipe on page 9. Transfer half the icing to another bowl and tint using the pink food colouring paste. Tint the other half violet. Fill a disposable piping bag with 3 tablespoons of the pink icing. Take some of the cookies and pipe outlines around each one. (See page 9 for instructions on flooding.) Add more pink colouring paste to the remaining pink icing to make a deeper shade, if you like, and pipe outlines around more cookies. Take another piping bag and spoon 3 tablespoons of the violet icing into it. Pipe an outline around the remaining cookies with the violet icing. Allow the icing to set for 10 minutes. Flood the insides of the outlines with a corresponding or contrasting colour. Allow to dry for 20 minutes. Pipe decorative patterns in contrasting colours on each ornament and decorate with edible silver balls and edible glitter. Allow the icing to set completely before threading with fine ribbon, if using.

Basic Spiced Gingerbread (page 6)
plain/all-purpose flour, for rolling out
Royal Icing (page 9)
pink and violet food colouring pastes
edible metallic balls
assorted edible glitter

assorted Christmas ornament cutters
wooden skewer or cocktail stick/toothpick (optional)
baking sheets, lined with non-stick baking parchment
disposable piping bags
fine ribbon (optional)

makes 12–16

Basic Spiced Gingerbread (page 6)
plain/all-purpose flour, for rolling out
Royal Icing (page 9)
red and black food colouring pastes
white sugar sprinkles

20-cm/8-inch-tall gingerbread-man cutter
baking sheets, lined with non-stick baking
   parchment
disposable piping bags

makes about 6

I have used an extra-large, simple gingerbread-man cutter to make these cute Santa cookies. The icing is slightly more fiddly than most cookies, but the recipe only makes 6 cookies, so it's quite manageable!

santa claus

Prepare the Basic Spiced Gingerbread according to the recipe on page 6, stopping at the end of Step 3. Preheat the oven to 170°C (325°F) Gas 3.

Lightly dust a clean, dry surface with flour and roll the dough evenly to a thickness of 2–3 mm/⅛ inch. Use the cutters to stamp out as many cookies as possible from the dough, cutting each one as close as possible to the next one. Arrange the cookies on the prepared baking sheets. Gather the dough scraps together, knead lightly, re-roll and stamp out more cookies until all the dough has been used up. Bake the gingerbread in batches on the middle shelf of the preheated oven for 10–12 minutes or until firm and lightly browned at the edges. Allow the cookies to cool completely on the baking sheets before icing.

Prepare the Royal Icing according to the recipe on page 9. Spoon three quarters of the icing into another bowl and tint a deep red colour using the food colouring paste. Tint a further 3 tablespoons black in a small bowl. Leave the remaining icing white. Fill a disposable piping bag with 2 tablespoons of the red icing and pipe an outline around the bottom half of each man in the shape of a pair of trousers. (See page 9 for instructions on flooding.) Do the same in a jacket shape around the top half. Pipe an outline for a hat. Fill another piping bag with the black icing and pipe an outline for the boots. Fill another piping bag with the white icing and pipe outlines for the fur trim on the hat, collar, belt, and sleeve and trouser cuffs. Allow to dry for at least 10 minutes.

Flood the white outlines with white icing, then scatter the white sugar sprinkles over these areas. Flood the remaining areas with their corresponding colours. Allow to dry for 20 minutes. Finally, pipe white buttons down the middle of Santa's jacket, a black buckle on his belt and 2 eyes and a big red nose. Allow to dry completely before serving.

Thread festive ribbons through these cookies so that they can be hung on a Christmas tree. Piping leaves is very easy but does require a special leaf icing tip or nozzle. You can also make leaves using fondant icing.

christmas wreaths

Prepare the Chocolate Gingerbread according to the recipe on page 7, stopping at the end of Step 3. Preheat the oven to 170°C (325°F) Gas 3.

Lightly dust a clean, dry surface with flour and roll the dough evenly to a thickness of 2–3 mm/⅛ inch. Using the larger cookie cutter, stamp out discs and arrange on the prepared baking sheets, spacing the cookies apart. Use the smaller cutter to stamp out discs from the middle of each cookie. Gather the dough scraps together, knead lightly, re-roll and stamp out more cookies until all the dough has been used up. Bake the gingerbread in batches on the middle shelf of the preheated oven for 10–12 minutes or until firm and browned at the edges. Allow the cookies to cool completely on the baking sheets before icing.

Prepare the Royal Icing according to the recipe on page 9. Divide the icing between 3 bowls. Tint 2 of the bowls different shades of green. Thicken each one by beating it vigorously for a minute or by adding more icing/confectioners' sugar. Leave the remaining bowl of icing white. Fill a disposable piping bag with about 4 teaspoons of one green icing and pipe an outline around the outside and inside edges of each cookie. (See page 9 for instructions on flooding.) Allow to dry for at least 10 minutes.

Flood the outlines with white icing. Allow to dry for 20 minutes.

Fit a piping bag with the leaf nozzle and fill with one shade of green icing. Pipe leaf shapes over the white icing. Repeat with the other shade of green icing until you have full, leafy wreaths. Dust with edible glitter. Tint the remaining white icing red, spoon into another piping bag and pipe small holly berries among the leaves. Allow the icing to set completely before threading with ribbon.

Chocolate Gingerbread (page 7)
plain/all-purpose flour, for rolling out
Royal Icing (page 9)
green and red food colouring pastes
edible green glitter

round fluted cookie cutters, 8 cm/3 inches and 3 cm/1 inch
baking sheets, lined with non-stick baking parchment
disposable piping bags
small leaf-shaped piping nozzle/tip
assorted ribbons

makes 12–14

I love baking treats for Christmas – for decorating the house, for gifts and for eating. These snowflakes tick all 3 boxes. Not only do they taste great, but they look stunning hung from silvery, frosty branches.

snowflakes

Basic Spiced Gingerbread (page 6)
plain/all-purpose flour, for rolling out
icing/confectioners' sugar, for rolling out
250 g/8 oz. ready-to-use fondant icing
2 tablespoons apricot jam, warmed and sieved/strained
4 tablespoons Royal Icing (page 9)
edible metallic balls

assorted snowflake cutters
baking sheets, lined with non-stick baking parchment
disposable piping bag
tiny star-shaped embossing tools

makes 10–16

Prepare the Basic Spiced Gingerbread according to the recipe on page 6, stopping at the end of Step 3. Preheat the oven to 170°C (325°F) Gas 3.

Lightly dust a clean, dry surface with flour and roll the dough evenly to a thickness of 2–3 mm/⅛ inch. Use the cutters to stamp out as many cookies as possible from the dough, cutting each one as close as possible to the next one. Arrange the cookies on the prepared baking sheets. Gather the dough scraps together, knead lightly, re-roll and stamp out more cookies until all the dough has been used up. Bake the gingerbread in batches on the middle shelf of the preheated oven for 10–12 minutes or until firm and lightly browned at the edges. Allow the cookies to cool completely on the baking sheets before icing.

Lightly dust the work surface with icing/confectioners' sugar and roll out the fondant icing to a thickness of no more than 2 mm/¹⁄₁₆ inch. Using the same snowflake cutters as above, stamp out shapes from the icing to match your cookies. Brush warmed apricot jam lightly over each cookie and carefully position the fondant snowflakes on top. Gently press the fondant snowflakes in place.

Prepare just 4 tablespoons of the Royal Icing according to the recipe on page 9. Fill the piping bag with the royal icing and pipe delicate lines across some of the snowflakes. Use the embossing tool to press delicate patterns into the fondant icing. Stick edible metallic balls to the snowflakes with a dot of royal icing. Allow the royal icing to set completely before threading the cookies with ribbon.

You won't need any fancy pumpkin-shaped cutters for these Halloween cookies, just a good dusting of orange sanding sugar and perhaps some ghoulish candies and jelly treats. Trick or treating just got way more fun.

jack-o'-lanterns

Prepare the Basic Spiced Gingerbread according to the recipe on page 6, stopping at the end of Step 3. Preheat the oven to 170°C (325°F) Gas 3.

Lightly dust a clean, dry surface with flour and roll the dough evenly to a thickness of 2–3 mm/⅛ inch. Use the cutters to stamp out as many cookies as possible from the dough, cutting each one as close as possible to the next one. Arrange the cookies on the prepared baking sheets. Gather the dough scraps together, knead lightly, re-roll and stamp out more cookies until all the dough has been used up. Bake the gingerbread in batches on the middle shelf of the preheated oven for 10–12 minutes or until firm and lightly browned at the edges. Allow the cookies to cool completely on the baking sheets before icing.

Prepare the Royal Icing according to the recipe on page 9. Spoon 1–2 tablespoons of the icing into a small bowl and tint green using the food colouring paste. Tint another 3 tablespoons of the icing black. Cover and set aside. Tint the remaining icing a deep shade of orange. Spoon 3 tablespoons of it into a disposable piping bag and pipe pumpkin-shaped outlines on each cookie. Use the green icing in the same way to make a stalk outline for each pumpkin. Allow to dry for at least 10 minutes. Flood the outlines with their corresponding colours. Allow to dry for just 5 minutes before dusting the pumpkin shape with orange sanding sugar. Allow to dry again for a further 15 minutes.

Pipe orange curved lines over each pumpkin. Allow to dry for 10–15 minutes before filling another piping bag with the black icing and piping eyes and spooky mouths onto each jack-o'-lantern. Allow to dry completely before serving.

Basic Spiced Gingerbread (page 6)
plain/all-purpose flour, for rolling out
Royal Icing (page 9)
green, black and orange food colouring pastes
orange sanding sugar

round cutter, about 9 cm/3⅝ inches
baking sheets, lined with non-stick baking parchment
disposable piping bags

makes 10–12

An unusual topper for a wedding cake perhaps, but if you've gone to the trouble of making your own cake, why stop there? Since you'll only need 2 people to go on top of the cake, use the leftover dough to make some love hearts from page 35 to complete the romantic theme.

bride & groom

Basic Spiced Gingerbread (page 6)
plain/all-purpose flour, for rolling out
Royal Icing (page 9)
black and yellow food colouring pastes

elegant gingerbread-man and -lady cutters
baking sheet, lined with non-stick baking parchment
disposable piping bags

makes 2 with plenty of leftover dough

Prepare the Basic Spiced Gingerbread according to the recipe on page 6, stopping at the end of Step 3. Preheat the oven to 170°C (325°F) Gas 3.

Lightly dust a clean, dry surface with flour and roll the dough evenly to a thickness of 2–3 mm/⅛ inch. Use the cutters to stamp out 2 (or more, in case any of them break or turn out wrong!) people from the dough. Arrange the cookies on the prepared baking sheet. Use the leftover dough to make any shapes you like. Bake the gingerbread on the middle shelf of the preheated oven for 10–12 minutes or until firm and lightly browned at the edges. Allow the cookies to cool completely on the baking sheet before icing.

Prepare the Royal Icing according to the recipe on page 9. Spoon half the icing into another bowl and tint black using the food colouring paste. Cover and set aside. Spoon 3 tablespoons of the white icing into a disposable piping bag and pipe an outline in the shape of a wedding dress around the bride cookie. Allow to dry for at least 10 minutes and then flood the middle of the dress with white icing. Allow to dry for 20 minutes while you dress the groom!

Spoon 3 tablespoons of the black icing into another piping bag and pipe an outline in the shape of a suit around the groom cookie. Pipe a triangle of white icing at the neck to make a shirt collar. Allow to dry for at least 10 minutes and then flood the middle of the suit with black icing and the collar with white icing. Allow to dry for 20 minutes.

To finish the bride and groom, pipe a decorative pattern in white icing over the wedding dress. Using the black icing, pipe lapels and jacket details on the groom cookie, including a cravat at the neck. Use the white icing to pipe a shirt collar. Finally, transfer a teaspoon of the remaining white icing into a small bowl and tint yellow using the food colouring paste. Fill another piping bag with the yellow icing and use to create a handkerchief in the groom's breast pocket.

Allow to dry completely before propping up on the wedding cake. Use the remaining dough and royal icing to make love-heart cookies or similar.

index